To Jennie and
Lou
my Friends

Patricia Meyer

To Jennie and Lou
my Friends
Patricia Mayer

DON'T DIE WONDERING;
Miracles Still Happen

**PATRICIA MEYER
LCSW**

Copyright © 2009 Patricia Meyer LCSW
All rights reserved.

ISBN: 1-4392-5512-1
ISBN-13: 9781439255124

Visit www.booksurge.com to order additional copies.

To Bill, without whose patience and computer skills this book would not have happened.

TABLE OF CONTENTS

CHAPTER 1. A FLEECY OMEN 1
CHAPTER 2. MY SPOOKY CHILDHOOD 3
CHAPTER 3. EARLY GOALS 7
CHAPTER 4. THE EMPTY NEST 13
CHAPTER 5. DON'T DIE WONDERING 17
CHAPTER 6. A BLESSING IN DISGUISE 23
CHAPTER 7. POSITIVE THINKING 27
CHAPTER 8. I GO PARANOID 29
CHAPTER 9. A MIRACULOUS NEAR MISS 35
CHAPTER 10. I JOIN THE CRISIS TEAM 37
CHAPTER 11. AN ESP EVENT 41
CHAPTER 12. THE MAILBOX EVENT 47
CHAPTER 13. THE DREAM 51
CHAPTER 14. PREDICTIVE DREAMS AND
 THE COLLECTIVE UNCONSCIOUS 55
CHAPTER 15. EDEN BECKONS 57
CHAPTER 16. CALIFORNIA HERE I COME 63
CHAPTER 17. GETTING SETTLED 67

CHAPTER 18.	THE WONDERS CONTINUE	71
CHAPTER 19.	ALL ROADS LEAD TO TIJUANA	73
CHAPTER 20.	LICENSING PROBLEMS	77
CHAPTER 21.	MY PROFESSIONAL DREAM IS FULFILLED	81
CHAPTER 22.	WONDERFUL SAN DIEGO	85
CHAPTER 23.	ANOTHER PREDICTIVE DREAM	89
CHAPTER 24.	I MOVE AGAIN	91
CHAPTER 25.	DREAMS DO COME TRUE	99
CHAPTER 26.	THE INCONVENIENT GRANDMOTHER	105
CHAPTER 27.	WE JOIN THE GLITTERATTI	107
CHAPTER 28.	WE FLY TO KEY WEST	115
CHAPTER 29.	CHRISTMAS IN HAWAII	119
CHAPTER 30.	BAD NEWS	125
CHAPTER 31.	WORSE NEWS	129
CHAPTER 32.	THE FUNERAL	133
CHAPTER 33.	I'VE HAD ENOUGH	135
CHAPTER 34.	EPILOGUE	141

Location: Heaven

Grandfather,

Well daughter, your youngest child has grown up, without your guidance and devotion. She was eleven years old when you joined us up here. She remembered your music instruction and has used it well, but her academic goals have been delayed. She is ambitious, she has talent… she is naïve. It's a tough world out there!

She will need our help.

* * *
Chapter 1
A FLEECY OMEN

The sky was a bit gray when we took off. I was returning to Indiana on a Braniff airplane, eager to tell my friends and coworkers about my marvelous adventures in California. When I looked up from my note taking I beheld a most wondrous sight. We were flying over...skimming over... an "ocean of whipped cream", with tall lumpy pillars of same reaching upward like church towers. The scene made me think of a song I learned in elementary school, "Silver argosies, ships of the air". The whipped cream clouds were deep and endless like a mattress of angel hair. The sun glistened on the whiteness like a snow scene, with the cloud towers appearing like ethereal snowmen. I was impressed by nature's amazing antics plus mankind's amazing technical skill which was able to place ME up above this snow cloud paradise.

Landing was of course inevitable and the workaday struggle soon to be resumed. I longed for "smooth sailing" in my professional life as well as in my personal life. My life had been scary, hectic, and – sometimes disappointing for the last 10 years. Efforts to shed one's skin and grow a new one had not been easy. I had been doing a complete makeover, reprogramming and renewing my mind through education and spiritual renewal. The beauty of the clouds appeared to me as an omen. Perhaps the lovely scene was about to become a reality. Soon I would finish my internship, pass the required testing (hopefully) and be on my way to my new life.. in California, where ` the sun always shines and unheard of dreams really do come true.'

When I reached my office my coworkers listened appreciatively to my story, (being trained therapists), and to my enthusiastic account of my glorious adventures. Then I sat down at my desk over which hung a picture of Dolores Del Rio, movie star. She was standing in the bougainvilla covered patio of her Spanish style Mexican home..."where the sun always shines." She seemed to be smiling down at me. I had a deep feeling of satisfaction that the smooth sailing I sought was on it's way.

* * *

* * *
Chapter 2
MY SPOOKY CHILDHOOD

When I was a kid I was scared of ghosts. Even the comic strips scared me because of a character in Popeye known as the Goon. He was large and white and shapeless. He was a ghost. He lived to eat hamburgers like his friend Wimpy, the fat man. At bedtime when my sisters finished brushing their teeth and fled down the stairs for their goodnight kisses I was left upstairs with goosebumps. Once when my sister's white night gown billowed out behind her I became hysterical, much to my mother's concern. Because of me she had to leave the hall light on all night for the next few years inflating the electric bill to my father's consternation. At grandmother's house, big, dark, and old, there was NO WAY I was going upstairs without a sister. I'd rather have an accident! Fortunately, one sister usually had to go too, so I had a companion. I was also a sleepwalker which annoyed my sister and scared my grandmother when I disappeared down the stairs when she left me in the upstairs hall while she readied the beds. I later learned this is called parasomnia and occurs during non-REM sleep; and that sleepwalkers are frequently psychic.

I was raised Methodist and was a believer. I tried to be a "good little girl" but I'm sure my long-suffering mother could tell you differently. I liked church and Sunday school because I felt safe there. They taught a Protective Power who would keep me safe. He would not go down the stairs leaving me alone and scared! I had my periods of negative and rebellious behavior and later on a period of weakness and failure. But I continued throughout my life to read and study a variety of religious., philosophical and self-help books, including comparative religions and metaphysics. I developed an interest in psychology. My mother died when I was 11 years old and that summer I beseeched the heavens to open a window so I could see her face once more: or perhaps let her speak to tell me WHY? But predictably no one answered. At that point I descended into what psychologists call dysthymia, a sort of chronic state of low- grade depression. In the late 30s we were still in the big depression and my father, an electrical engineer, had been unemployed for four years. There was no money for my mother's operation and health insurance had not yet been invented. I had no clothes for high school except for hand-me-downs from relatives and a high school friend! My sisters and I had no spending money except for a quarter which grandpa provided each week. Ironically it was just four years later, when I finished high school and went to work, that one of the first things my employer gave me was a Blue Cross card, followed by a Social Security number. Blue Cross four years earlier might have saved my mother's life.

In spite of the dysthymia which underlay the good times and the stresses of adolescence, I became a poet, writing philosophical and searching-for-answers types of poems. I discovered that music helped and I practiced the piano diligently every morning before the others were up (this habit received mixed reviews from late sleepers) My diligence was rewarded when at the age of eleven I played in a recital over St. Louis radio KWK on Sunday afternoon, on a program called the Baldwin hour.

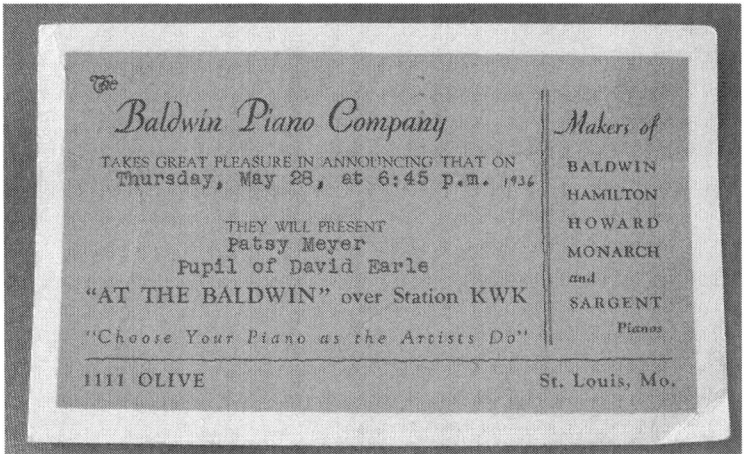

An annoucement from the Baldwin Piano hour.

By the time my sister and I graduated from high school my father chose to remodel our colonial residence into four apartments. Housing was scarce since World War II and rents were high. Dad had struggled for years to pay the mortgage on our home while we were in school and now he needed to make some money. I went to work as a cashier in a drive-in restaurant. The pay was low and I had no transportation. The buses stopped running at 1 AM and I was required to work later than that on weekends. A car hop who worked with me began driving me home. He was trying his luck in the real estate business but since he was new sales were slow. He had taken a course in accounting at Washington University but found it hard going and not his cup of tea. He had a great sense of humor and made me laugh. We decided we needed each other – for support and motivation as well as for love and transportation! Now, three sons and 28 years later everything was ending. My job had ended at the Department of Defense as the Vietnam War was winding down. The marriage had been a troubled one with differing world views and backgrounds. In spite of how we tried, including marriage counseling, things did not improve. By this time I had of course overcome my fear of ghosts!. but other fears had replaced them, like, how to manage a house and garden alone, how to earn a living large enough to pay the rent, my health insurance, and my car insurance, and how to protect myself out in the world. I hoped that protective power I'd learned about in Sunday School was real.

* * *

***
Chapter 3
EARLY GOALS

My Mother, who had been disappointed in her marriage and chagrined that she had married without first acquiring skills for earning a living, wanted a PhD for me. This because I had excelled in math and been pushed ahead two grades in elementary school. With her death and the depression, this dream vanished, as did my classical music lessons, ...since my father's fortunes were ruined by the depression and never really recovered. Back in 1941 my high school did not much bother with girls who could not afford college. There were no trained school counselors, and the possibility of a scholarship was not mentioned to me, a girl. My father did not attend to this issue because he believed college would be wasted on girls "who would just get married anyway". I had ranked in the upper 8% of my class without really trying since no one advised me of the various professions in the world of work or supported my goals. As a consequence, in my early jobs I always felt that I was in the wrong place. I worked as a typist, a clerk, a bookkeeping machine handle-puller, a telegraph operator, and a magazine market researcher. I was bored. I needed a challenge. I finally figured it out. Those young men they were hiring to do their "real" book keeping, and the real decision-making ... they had college...so during my marriage I began attending night classes at the local university college, teaching piano at home to earn the fees. I was 30 years old and this had only just become available. The University of Missouri at Columbia had opened a branch in St. Louis. Continuing education had thus been born. I worked on my BS for seven years at night school, transferring back to Washington University in my third year. During these years we bought a home, and then another, and raised three sons with their differing needs, talents and problems. Sometimes making a decision was hard as I'm sure everyone knows. (My father used to say "life is just one darn problem after another"! But remember "things are never so bad that they can't get worse.") How's that for mixed messages? I didn't know whether to be an optimist or a pessimist! Then I discovered hunches. I had learned decision-making by weighing all the pros and cons of a situation but I discovered, when trying to make a decision about buying a certain house, that my "gut feeling" gave me the right answer. This, I decided, worked because it is not possible to know all the pros and cons of a situation. This made me think about hunches and guidance. Religious literature is full of guidance; we pray for it, yearn for it, but how do we know when we're getting it? Is it "the still, small voice"? No that's conscience, – you usually know when you're doing something wrong,– but guidance? How does it occur, how does it feel? Is it about timely coincidences? Sudden insights? Clarity of thought? Inspiration? (I believe that's how those men of old wrote the Bible... a sudden inspiration, a sudden knowing so clear and wise it needed to be written down.) Anyhow that is my interpretation. Then there is intuition. Where does that come from? For a long time I ignored those intuitive messages and stuck with logic. Then I began to listen. I was finding that every time I ignored a hunch, I ended up doing the wrong thing. Does the FORCE really talk to us? Is there a consciousness in the heavens which is in touch with us? – Jesus said "I am the vine... you are the branches"- hence we are connected. I had decided to major in math since Monsanto was advertising for "women with math courses". However I discovered math skills fade with age if not used. Having struggled through trigonometry I decided to change my major to psychology, which seemed to be a better path, considering my religious and philosophical interests. In studying psychology I was thrilled to learn about famous and learned men who had interesting ideas about the things I was interested in. For instance, Carl Jung, an important psychologist and student of Sigmund Freud who studied consciousness, gave us the concept of the "collective unconscious," a meeting of individual unconscious thought which can be shared. The concept sounds to me something like the Akashic records or "book of life", – a religious concept from ancient Hinduism in which all is recorded. Edgar Casey, the Virginia Beach phenomenon - also known as the Sleeping Prophet – was able to go into a trance and diagnose people concerning their health and treatments, after being given only their addresses. His readings were recorded by helpers and he never charged a cent. His readings often cured where doctors had failed. He did a lot of good, but died in 1945, from overwork, trying to help too many people during and after World War II. His Institute still functions in Virginia Beach and his books are still in print. It was felt he was able to tap into the great unconscious. This may sound strange but what is prayer besides tapping into a higher power? Many people believe in saints and angels as connections to Heaven, doing the helping job. A modern psychologist Dean Radin PhD has written a book called "The Conscious Universe".* Dr. Radin is the Director of the Consciousness Research laboratory at the University of Nevada, Las Vegas, and formerly with

Princeton's Department of psychology. He has done cutting-edge research and experimentation in parapsychology for AT&T, Contel, and the U.S government. I love the idea of a conscious universe alive and aware and concerned with us, rather than the concept of empty space out there.

In 1909 William James, a Harvard University psychologist wrote that he was convinced of "super normal knowledge which exists in a common reservoir of consciousness."

Everyone has an unconscious which affects all we do. Ancient unconscious groupings are known as Arch Types, defined as common needs and motivations of humanity. These were featured some years ago on TV by Joseph Campbell:.. and provide us with another overarching connection with the lives of the many who preceded us. My interest in getting answers I believe began with the trauma of the early loss of my mother, although many if not most people begin to wonder about the unknown at some time in their lives. I hoped my mother was rejoicing somewhere at my late-bloomer attempts to use my early promise working toward a worthwhile career of helping others as well as helping myself.

*HarperEdge (1997)

* * *

Chapter 4
THE EMPTY NEST

"Or watch the things you gave your life to, broken[1]
And stoop and build them up with worn out tools"

My job ended at the Defense Department as the Vietnam War was winding down.. The boys were grown and mostly gone. My husband's business was failing, big time... and the marriage was too. It had been an unfulfilling time and we both were ready for a change...so,... midlife crisis for two. He wanted more chemistry in the relationship, "all or nothing at all," you might say, and I wanted the freedom to seek my lost dreams. We decided at long last to seek what we had been missing. It was a hard and scary decision. My youngest son decided to live with his father. My second son had married and moved to

---

[1] IF by Rudyard Kipling

South County. My oldest son was away in the military. I didn't know how I would make a living teaching elementary piano and besides I wanted more than that. Since my husband's business had failed we were broke. The future looked grim. I didn't know "what kind of work I was out of". I was depressed. You can't walk away from that many years and not care. I felt like not going on – – not trying anymore. I got down on my knees and prayed "dear God, if you are there, speak to me now."

Then an unusual book came into my possession. I had always been interested in the study of psychology. I had read several popular self-help books, including Karen Horney's book on self-analysis. I devotedly followed magazine articles such as " Can this marriage be saved?" written by Paul Popenoe.[2] I wanted very much to learn about marriage therapy and child raising. Better late than never, right? I wanted self- knowledge which I could also use to help others who may have been as mystified as I. But back to the unusual book. It was written by Frederick Perls, the famous Gestalt therapist of Big Sur, California. It ended by asking if you would like to be a gestalt therapist, and gave the number to call for more information.

Yes I would LOVE to be a Gestalt therapist. But could I afford to spend my nest egg? Would I be employable as a beginner at more than 50 years old? Would a grad

---

[2] Paul Popenoe Ladies Home Journal

school accept me? A tough decision! Friends and relatives thought me foolish. "You had your chance" the delivery man said. "My Aunt's now a professional student" was my nephew's opinion. Then I came across a feature in the newspaper about a 50-year-old woman on the East Coast who decided she wanted to be an MD. She had five or six children and had to commute to Chicago for her courses of study. Her husband was cooperative and agreed to attend to the children. (I hope there was a grandmother available!) I decided if she could do it, so could I. But of course doubts crept in occasionally. Then one day while browsing through a flea market, -which I very seldom did,- I came across a large button which stated the following piece of wisdom, DONT DIE WONDERING. Was that from above or what? Some say there are no coincidences. Was that guidance? I decided to DO or DIE. . I took the risk and signed up, committing almost my last cent for my last chance. I found a local university class especially for "displaced homemakers". This was in the 1960s when divorce was becoming rampant and many full-time homemakers were suddenly out on their own. These students would be about my age and so more comfortable for me. I planned to complete my undergraduate degree there. Due to good design in an Experimental Psychology class experiment that the professor especially liked, I was given a referral to another wonderful Ivy League university for their 3/2 program which allows a student to do two semesters in one of undergraduate work, namely Washington U. I sent in my application for graduate work in psychology and social work. I was accepted! Amen. Oh yes, I had to do eight hours of testing first. I passed!

* * *

Chapter 5
DON'T DIE WONDERING

I was thrilled but also scared to death. With all those brilliant young people who would be my classmates, I was also a little paranoid. Would I look foolish at my age? Would my comment sounds stupid? (Class participation was required) Would they laugh at me? Well Jesus told the fisherman (if you're not having any luck,) "cast your nets in deeper water".

I made it through orientation week on January 16 both nervous and excited, and headed for the parking lot, which was down two long, wide flights of concrete steps with an iron railing on the left side. It had been snowing. There was ice at the top of the stairs which I attempted to jump over. I slipped, and fell head first, the concrete corners of the steps pointing at my head. I struggled to get my feet under me, succeeded, and landed full weight on them and broke both feet. I sprained my ankle and badly wrenched a knee. As I sat there dazed and embarrassed and wondering if I had blown it all, my mother's voice came to me clearly. It said "Trust me Patsy, it's in my hands"! No one had called me Patsy except my mother.! It's in her hands? I was stunned. So stunned that I later wrote it down and I still have that slip of paper in one of my old pocketbooks. I slid on my bottom over to the left railing, somehow stood up enough to hang my stomach over it, and more or less slid down two flights to my car. I removed my shoes from my throbbing feet and headed for home, – a 45 minute drive. When I arrived home my feet were so swollen I could not put on my shoes. I crawled along the porch on my hands and knees, opened the front door and crawled up the split level steps from the foyer to the living room.

A phone hung on the kitchen wall and I had to stand to use it. I called my husband who had started a new job nearby. His boss's wife answered and told me my husband was making a big sale with a new customer and couldn't be disturbed. I told her my problem and she said "I'll be right there". She was, and when she saw me standing with the phone she said "get off those feet or you'll never walk again"!. I did. The rest, as you can imagine was hard. My son, whom I had called next, who worked nearby managing a candy store, was so upset he mistakenly drove all the way over to Washington University looking for me before he remembered I had called from home. He took me to the ER. where casts were applied to both legs. I was weeping over my lost scholarship but the doctor said to my son "any one who starts a new career requiring advanced degrees at age 50, is not going to let a broken leg get in the way".

The magic button found at the flea market

* * *

"He who started a good work in you, will also do it!"
Phil. 1:36

Chapter 6
A BLESSING IN DISGUISE

My entry into grad school and my 3/2 scholarship had to be postponed until the summer session. The powers that be urged me to continue NOW but I could not imagine myself at my age stumbling up the steps to class and the third floor library with two crutches and a heavy book bag on my back. Granted the semester reprieve, I was confined pretty much to my bed for a few weeks. Eventually I hobbled across the hall and resumed teaching piano to a favorite few. My best friend on the block came by every morning bringing me coffee and rolls. Fortunately she worked nearby at an aircraft plant and so returned at lunchtime with a McDonald hamburger and fries. In time she began taking me to her beauty salon, which I sorely needed. Next came church. My friend had found a minister who "really turner her on" and she was not embarrassed to haul me around with one leg in a cast and the other in a bandage, with two crutches. She had been "born again" and had experienced a whole new take on life. She had not been raised with any religious instruction. Because she was so newly inspired, she came by often to do Bible study with me. Nevertheless I was lonely and my bed felt empty at night. I'd wake and reach out...but it was empty. One night I heard a loud "crack". WHAT WAS THAT? Later I learned it was the foundation and the outer wall of the family room that had split a bit due to the sloping lot. It had shifted in the rain storms we were having. Another night I awoke with a start. The bedroom wall, the one across from the long wide windows was a flaming scarlet. Must be a fabulous sunrise, I thought. I turned toward the windows. They were dark, as dark as two AM, which is what it was. I went back to sleep, wondering.

After my fall I wondered "why did this happen NOW?" Why did God, if he cared for me., if there IS a God, allow this NOW? Three months later, with my friend's grounding me in appropriate and affirmative scriptures, I realized how much stronger I was. Without it I would never have made it through the next two years. I have wondered, am I really meant to do this? Why me? A scripture one Sunday morning gave me the answer —"The fields are white, the harvests are plentiful, but the laborers are few". I figured they must need me. As a matter of fact, a year into my masters degree I was required to do an internship and to find one for myself if possible. This very church sponsored and managed a children's home in a nearby neighborhood which sheltered a range of children from five to late adolescence, many from the inner city. The social worker in charge who was also from my school, hired me and I learned a great deal from this position. They were short of everything there and I was, among other duties, in charge of phoning companies and charities and whomever for needed supplies. I realized "the harvest really needed me."

* * *

Chapter 7
POSITIVE THINKING

"It's the attitude that counts". That's what my young son used to say. Where this bit of wisdom came from I couldn't say but I suspected he must've heard some domestic squabbling from time to time between my husband and me. Occasionally, if he heard us "debating," he would remind us, "it's the attitude that counts"! Optimism in overcoming obstacles and setbacks is a must! "When the going gets tough, the tough get going" per Dr. Robert Schuller, of the Chrystal Cathedral in Garden Grove Ca., (although it is also necessary to have a plan B,.. my note.) Your presentation of yourself, your respect for others, your self-confidence, your belief in what you're doing, and yes your belief in Providence will all open doors for you. (Faith can move mountains!) During my studies I learned that the very effective 12 steps programs, AA and

NA for treating alcohol and drug addictions, work best because they make use of the Higher Power concept. They work better than any other therapeutic intervention.

Goethe, the famous German philosopher wrote "When you take a bold step the universe moves to support you". Isn't that astounding? I was glad to find that. Words are important; they can change your life. Words like these make one think about the consciousness of the universe for this help must come from somewhere. As I soldiered on with my life I found both of these things to be true.

* * *

Chapter 8
I GO PARANOID

I began again in the June semester. I was of course thrilled to be accepted at this wonderful university and that was probably why I was so scared. Would I measure up? Would the other students think I was too old? I became self-conscious. I would sweat if anyone looked at me over long. I was experiencing social anxiety. In one class we had to choose partners for a project. I was chosen last. During the lecture a young lady stared at me a lot, with what I perceived (probably wrongly) as a hostile expression. I was worried that if they knew I had been treated for depression (at the end of my marriage) and had seen a therapist for it that it would go against me, especially in the line of work I was heading for, which was mental health. After all, my entire future depended on my new plans working out. I discovered later that this experience helped rather than hurt, but at the time I didn't know that. So I avoided her staring eyes, but after a while I began to get angry. I looked directly into her eyes with a great deal of fear and hostility of my own. As our eyes met, the instructor's large, un- occupied wooden desk chair moved and banged loudly against the desk. Everyone jumped. The professor said "what the devil was that?" Several students, including myself went forward and examined the chair and desk. No clues were found. The teacher said "come on forget it, let's get back to work".

I now know that this was psychokineses—a psychic state which moves objects. Some teenagers have been known to have this ability and move objects around the house. It is thought that it is sometimes an emotional disturbance in the teenagers which allows this to happen. Psychokinesis has been defined as "mentally causing action at a distance". It apparently requires strong emotion to bring this about. In this case it was apparently the force of a deep negative emotion. I was a psychology major. I decided to apply 'thought substitution' (which I had learned as a treatment for depression called Cognitive Therapy) to erase the unhelpful negative thoughts I was thinking,– and it worked. The next morning when I passed a young woman coming up the walk I said to myself, "isn't she pretty – looks nice – looks friendly – might like a smile". This worked beautifully and I got a big smile in return.

We students were instructed to do ESP experiments in an early class, trying to convey playing card numbers and suits, by concentration, to a receiving person in another room. This proved to be "statistically significant" (successful) at times, meaning the correct receptions were above the average law of chance. Several well-known scientists have been doing experiments for many years and it has been proven beyond a doubt that psychic transference exists. On a related subject, interestingly, one psychologist I read wrote about somnambulance, which is sleep walking.. He stated that sleepwalkers usually display a range of paranormal skills. I was a sleep walker! I had scared my grandmother when I was a child and my sister. I'm glad I was not living in the 16th century! I would really hate being burned as a witch.! Scientists tell us that somnambulism occurs during non-Rem sleep, another activity of the brain which we formerly knew little about.

* * *

"He shall give his angels charge over you."
Psalms 91:10-11

Chapter 9
A MIRACULOUS NEAR MISS

In due time I graduated and sent out resumes far and wide – to Florida, Indiana, and California, and yes, Missouri. I wanted a new scene, preferably one with continual sunshine. However I learned that the government had financed new community mental health centers in some states. I landed a great job in Indiana working as a generalist therapist plus crisis work, not easy but an advantageous and instructive beginning. I stayed for three years to fulfill the supervision requirements for taking the social worker "bar exam", and get certified. I was only 500 or so miles from home, and did receive visits from my sister and my son and daughter-in-law. But when Christmas came I looked forward to visiting home. I shopped for lovely gifts for all which were much better than I could normally afford, including new sweaters for the boys. I hoped the oldest would be able to get home on leave. I left a department store in Ft. Wayne and headed down Highway 1, for my more rural address. I worked in a central office and also the branch office. I lived near the branch clinic. It was just dark when I turned down Highway 1. It was a two lane road., one lane in each direction, with frequent culverts with stone protectors along the way. There was very little shoulder available for pulling off. Suddenly my late father's voice said clearly "Keep your car under control". I did often drive with a "heavy foot" on the gas, so I slowed way down to 35 or 40 mph. In a short while I saw two headlights coming **RIGHT AT ME** on my side of the road. I stomped on the brake and moved only inches to the right, because of the stone abutments. The other driver "came to" and swerved right. He/she missed me by inches! Not my time eh? Providence must have wanted those sweaters delivered! And my dad's voice..wow..who knew they watched us from above? Well I survived and delivered the sweaters. We had a nice Christmas and yes all three sons were there and me too, thanks to unexpected help out of the blue.

* * *

Chapter 10
LIFE ON THE CRISIS TEAM

As a generalist therapist I was required to take my turn on the crisis team. This involved being available 24 hours for any call that came in. My first assignment was to go to the local fair and talk a man down off of a roof, since he was planning to jump. I reviewed my notes on suicide and went and did the job. He did not jump; he came down and talked with me until I deemed him safe and then made an appointment for further treatment. It was hard to believe that this was ME, doing this work. What a change! Next I went out with the crisis team to a rural farm home. There a woman had locked herself in the bathroom where she was suspected by family members of taking too many pills. Our job was to talk her out of the bathroom but the husband didn't want our help and he possessed a shotgun. I was warned by my team to try to "stay behind a tree", as you never knew when a gun might protrude from any window. Eventually, persuasion did the job. Ultimately I declined an offer to accept a permanent place on the crisis team. A third assignment involved a young woman who reported abuse from her boyfriend. She was afraid to leave him and afraid not to do whatever he commanded. Yet she came to the Center for help and was assigned to me where I worked to strengthen her confidence as I tried to get her into a women's shelter. The office staff liked to have lunch together at a town restaurant with a back room bar and game room, such as for shooting pool. One day I looked up from my lunch to see this woman's boyfriend staring, glaring at me from that room. It made me shiver. About a week later I woke suddenly at night and sat straight up. I was filled with terror. All was quiet; then I heard a rustling sound. I wanted to phone for help but I couldn't move. I was frozen like a deer in the headlights. My upstairs neighbor was out of town and the older lady in the small studio had moved out. I was alone in the building. After awhile I unfroze enough to reach the phone next to the bed and I tried to dial out. It was disconnected!

I grabbed my pillow and ran to the walk-in pantry, locked the door and finally fell asleep on the floor. The next morning all was well. Nothing bad had happened. The phone company reported that there had been trouble on the line the night before. This event hurried my decision to move west as soon as my qualifications were acquired. That night, still on the crisis team, I had a late call out and when I returned home I was very tired and my eyes hurt. I reached under the bathroom washbowl for a large bottle of pure water and quickly poured it into an old-fashioned eye cup– one my grandmother had left me – for bathing the eyes. I was eager to get to bed so I quickly dashed it into my left eye. There was another bottle of the same size under the wash bowl which sat next to the water bottle and it contained bleach. You guessed it,– I had bleached my eye.

In a panic I filled the wash bowl with pure water and stuck my head in it submerging that eye. I could barely reach the phone but I finally did manage to reach it and called the doctor, who arrived in 10 minutes. He dripped water through the affected eye for 20 minutes before moving me to the hospital. Then I called my son in St. Louis who was to meet me tomorrow in Chicago and together we would fly to visit son number one and his wife in San Francisco. The water treatment went on through the night and by morning I was able to don a black eye patch, receive special eye drops, go home and get my mostly packed suitcase and head for the airport. I connected with my St. Louis son in Chicago and together we made it to San Francisco, having orders from my MD to seek out an ophthalmologists once there. So, having done crises all week I now had created one of my own.!

Richard, (son number 1) and his wife went to work and Paul (son number 3) and I took a bus to my eye appointment. The bus stopped at Golden Gate Park. It was crowded, with standing room only. I stood in the aisle and clung to a post as a group of rowdy teenagers boarded and pushed their way through. A fight broke out in the aisle, and I was shoved and my head banged into the post, rattling my eyes. The driver brought the bus to a halt and several troublemakers were forced to disembark. I made it to my appointment and my eye was okay. I am happy to be able to report that the rest of the San Francisco vacation was a "hoot" and a dream. How could it not be when Rich had retired from the service and they were now living in beautiful Sausalito?

* * *

Chapter 11
AN ESP EVENT

It was a pleasant Saturday and I was bound to spend the day studying and reviewing, preparing for the BIG TEST in Indianapolis, the state certification exam. I worked on my rented front porch which was enclosed with jalousie windows. I crammed for eight solid hours reviewing two years of college work. Suddenly I realized "I've got it. It's all come together. I SEE the whole picture. I see how it works! I'm going to make it!" Suddenly the porch seemed to glow, to light up, very bright, although the sun was already shining. The plants and flowers and trees looked great! Extra colorful. I felt high (the colors, the colors)! but without any chemical help! It was an alpha experience,—like Barbra Streisand's recording of "On a Clear Day"[3] which really describes the "alpha" state since

---

[3] From the movie Bridey Murphy

you feel part of a larger world or hear sounds or see intense colors you've never heard or seen -that's how I felt! My number one son was in Monterey, California with his wife and in-laws, visiting from Florida. He was bored, he said, idly looking at "tourist stuff" when, (he wrote in his letter), "mom it was like you were right there beside me! I looked down and saw this souvenir package of little box matches in different colors. They said, "success, love, respect, happiness, good fortune, peace, etc." They said what he wished for me, in my new beginnings. Joy. Our mutually elevated emotions, strong emotions, (he cared about me), must have met across 2000 miles. He sent me the matches. I still have them, – (the ones that a friend didn't accidentally use) – and then we compared the time. I finished my studies at 3:30 PM in Indiana; and he and the family were browsing, having just finished lunch at 1:30 PM California time, which is of course two hours earlier than Indiana time.!

AN ESP EVENT

These are the matches my son sent which inspired the ESP event.

What causes ESP? There are many recorded anecdotal events concerning paranormal happenings. In fact, another girlfriend of mine had a similar experience. She was sleeping but woke and sat straight up at midnight. She saw headlights coming straight for a car resulting in a terrible collision. A young teenager was killed and she turned out to be her son's little 16 year old girlfriend. The entire church congregation and neighborhood grieved. But my friend saw it before the phone rang!. But I digress. There are thousands of anecdotal stories of paranormal events such as ESP, precognition, predictive dreams, and psychokinesis.

So I decided to research this phenomena beginning with finding information and books online. I was surprised how many scientific experiments have been performed in this area, for many generations!, including at well known and respected universities.

Having finished school and graduated I began canvassing churches and the community college looking for space or a job teaching my classes, particularly parent education or family communications. I preferred to be employed in an agency since I liked working with colleagues. I needed companions. I wanted to be part of a group. Then I had another dream, or was it a vision? Let's call it an unusual visual happening. I woke up in the morning and sat there gazing out the window. I saw dimly a group of eight people, head and shoulders, smiling at me. As I stared, it faded. When I got my job in Indiana, it was in a small office composed of 8 friendly people. We all had lunch together.!

My sister and I decided to take a little vacation trip, down to the beautiful Ozarks in southern Missouri. Just a long weekend. I thought we should visit our father living in Sedalia just west of Jefferson City. With his wife in the hospital he was all alone. Plans did not go that way however, since the boys, my kids and my nephews, needed to get back and didn't want to miss out on water skiing. One lovely evening my sister and I sat on the deck gazing at the lake. The boys had gone into town to visit the "Dog Patch" a tourist attraction Then there came a SHOT and I jumped up. "What was THAT?: I asked.

My sister said she hadn't really heard anything, "But the boys went into town" I said "and this SOUND came from next door, the boys' unit!" We checked. A large plastic raft had fallen down, not a sharp noise, but I had heard it as a shot. In five days, back home in St. Louis we received a phone call. My father was found dead. Neighbors reported hearing a shot. After five days the body was found, but was too far decomposed to autopsy.

* * *

Chapter 12
THE MAILBOX EVENT

After completing our three years of supervision, my colleagues and I went to Indianapolis and took the Certification exam. We were excited, and somewhat worried, since our futures were at stake. When will the results come? It was hard waiting. One morning I was at the clinic seeing clients as usual but I was eager for lunchtime. I wanted to get home. I knew—just KNEW the test results were in my mailbox. I told my fellow therapist, and he said "yeh, right". Lunchtime came and I walked home (I lived two blocks from the clinic) and there, – you guessed it, – were the test results (I passed) and my Certification! I was now an ACSW, an Accredited clinical social worker. How did I know the test results were there? A hunch? Intuition? Clairvoyance? Where does it come from? How did I become a 'sensitive' if that's what I am?

California was my goal. My long-time high school girlfriend from St. Louis was doing well there in the real estate business. She had asked me to come out so that we "could retire together". I wasn't exactly ready to retire, but I did hope to return to the wonderland I had visited when I was 19 years old. I still had a house sitting in St. Louis County, rented out, and I knew it would be best to sell it before moving cross – country. Alas the times were NOT right. It was the 70s, when inflation had gone rampant and loan money was almost non-existent. Interest rates had climbed to 14 and 16%! Banks were giving away crock pots and sandwich toasters just to get your cash deposit. The interest rates helped my savings, but when it came to real estate sales, it was strictly a buyers market. FHA loans were hard to come by unless the buyer had good credit and the house had to be in great shape. Oh my broken foundation! Oh the mud that had washed over the basement door step as never before, due to torrential rains and snow that year.

Months went by and I worried. How would I buy in California without this sale? I hated to leave the house in the hands of an agent, and since my former neighbor had called me twice about kids putting snow in the dining room (I supposed a looker must've left the door unlatched) and one time she thought my tenant was moving out. That proved to be a false alarm. It was a friend moving in with my present tenant. I authorized my agent to have done all the repairs required by the FHA and I waited and prayed. When dozing in my chair after the 10 o'clock news, about ready to go to bed I saw a ball of light – very bright, almost blue-white, about the size of a grapefruit or a fourth of July sparkler. It was moving down the hall of my St. Louis house, about 3 feet off floor, into the den, and out, then into the small bedroom and into the master bedroom, the kitchen and the family room. Was it someone who loved the house? Had I been dreaming? The next day I called my real estate person and she told me she had shown the house the night before to a customer who was very enthusiastic about it. I took the moving light as a sign,... to sell the house at the 'low ball' price the customer had offered. Praise God the deal went through. I am now free to move about the country!

* * *

Chapter 13
THE DREAM

My son had recently left the service where he had been a Navy pilot for eight years. He was now employed by Braniff Airlines as first navigator and then copilot. I was very proud of him and happy for him since this had been his heart's desire since childhood. He was eager to do something for me, and encouraged me to take a trip or two. It was late spring. I was still working in Indiana. I had been reluctant to travel alone. All my office colleagues were talking about their forthcoming vacations, trips, and beach houses. I felt left out and wondered what to do with myself. Richard was urging me not to delay. One night I had a dream. Not an ordinary dream but the kind that is SO REAL that when you wake up you wonder, what does it MEAN? In my dream my son was standing beside a very large plane, a 747 I believe. He was smiling and beckoning urgently. It wasn't the urgency of a crisis exactly because he was smiling, – but HURRY! was conveyed. What did it mean? I decided to fly to England all by myself. I wanted a European vacation but was afraid to go to any country where they spoke a foreign language. I didn't want to have to do charades to find my hotel or the return airport for that matter! So I chose England. My son was glad and booked me with an "airline community group"., leaving from the airline's hub in Dallas. It was a wonderful time. I had never thought of England as such a beautiful and historically interesting place. It was 1981, the year Diana got married to the Royal Prince. London had been spiffed up with gold painted fence tops and such. A family of three on the plane adopted me. We made a foursome for dinner and while sightseeing. Their daughter was an ice skater training in Dallas for a professional or an Olympic career. They were very interesting people and it was a treat. I wouldn't have missed it for the world, except that I almost DID miss it. The dream which told me to "come on, hurry" - proved to be providential. It proved to be a precognitive dream. For in just a few weeks Braniff Airlines went into bankruptcy, and my son's airline career was over. Did he know? He didn't think he did. Was it a rumor which transferred to me? But according to a Braniff newsletter I read some years later, I found none of the staff knew. They found out when they came to work and discovered the planes stacked up at the gates! Or did I know on some deep subliminal level from "the collective unconscious of the universe"?

My son Richard flies for Braniff Airlines.

* * *

Chapter 14
PREDICTIVE DREAMS AND THE COLLECTIVE UNCONSCIOUS

Carl G. Jung, although originally a student of Sigmund Freud, deviated from Freud's Orthodox psychoanalytic theory. His concepts were influenced by Plato, the philosopher Schopenhauer, and Emanuel Kant's notion of "universal forms of perception". All of that preceded Jung's ideas of a "collective unconscious" (from which dreams may emerge?)(my note).

In The Talmud, the first five books of the Jewish Bible, a great deal of attention was given to dream interpretation. Dream interpretation as an expression of the unconscious was also important in Sigmund Freud's work.

I happily found the above information in a psychological textbooks used at the college level.

Dr. Dean Radin, PhD,[4] director of the current Consciousness Research laboratory at the University of Nevada, Las Vegas, speaks of a connected realm of consciousness, in his wonderful book The Conscious Universe; - when writing about the scientific truth of psychic phenomena..

Is this thinking so far out? Is this so different from conventional religion which tells us of the Spirit being alive and well and living 'up there' and in us? Or the older concept of saints and angels watching over us from above and directing our lives? Scientists who had thought space empty now know that it is far from empty, with dark energy and dark matter out there. It is not on our wavelength of visibility, but... it's there.

* * *

---

[4] Harper Edge 1997

Chapter 15
EDEN BECKONS

My last winter in Indiana was the most severe. My car had been buried at the curb for six weeks. The city snowplow cleared the snow somewhat from the street in front of my house/apartment, throwing ice and snow up over my car. Temperatures were at 10°F. I tried to hire someone to shovel me out, but no go. Too hard. So I took up walking, which was no doubt better for my health and figure anyway. Then two days after Christmas I made a trip to San Diego California to see my long time girlfriend, and to see what my prospects might be like out there. When I deplaned on December 27 wearing my heavy coat and boots, the air was like spring. I exclaimed to my friend who met me, "Nan, it's like April here! She responded with a casual "oh yeah, it's always like that!" Later I learned San Diegans get up in the morning saying "ho-hum, another perfect day in paradise!" Since Nancy was in real estate sales I agreed to go with her on her Monday morning rounds where the salesperson's view what everyone else has listed for sale over the weekend. And transfixed by it all I bought a condo! How could I resist? It faced on a beautiful heated swimming pool; it was next-door to the clubhouse, the laundry and the sauna. Blooming at my front door were gardenias, geraniums, (they grow like weeds out there) and a scarlet blooming bottle brush tree. Bird of Paradise adorned the pool area. Johnny-jump-ups sprang up out of cracks in the sidewalk or driveway, so abundant was life in California. I couldn't go away without buying something could I? I placed a down payment. I needed a loan so I took a 2 year balloon note, hoping my St. Louis house sale would be coming through soon. I sat next to my friend's desk and went into a trance of deep thought, with an emotionless stare. What had I done? Two of my sons and my sisters were in St. Louis! But son number one was in Texas with a prospect of marrying and moving out here. I heard my friend and sales agent call out to her colleagues "look, she's got buyer's remorse!" But no good things come without taking a risk, I decided. And remember, Jesus told the fishermen "Cast your nets in deeper water" (and you'll catch more fish.) I needed to catch a lot of fish to get my retirement nest egg up to snuff.

I discovered I'd have to take two more licensing exams – one written and one oral, – plus return to school for two or three courses in Human Sexuality. Since there was an early

80s recession happening I might have to go into private practice if I couldn't find a job. Friends in Indiana had so warned me but somehow I had turned a deaf ear. The following June I caught a plane for San Diego carrying two cats, a sleeping bag, a leather coat, three pieces of luggage (2 checked through), a purse and a book bag around my neck carrying the contents of my safe deposit box. The cat litter, pans and food were in a suitcase (with a small rubber tree which I had used for my Christmas tree in Indiana)! My ex had agreed to buy my old Cadillac and so drove up from St. Louis to claim it and to drive me to the Indianapolis airport. We stopped at the DMV to make the transfer. It was hot and the cats didn't like being in their cages during this delay. On the way again I stuck my hand into the cages to comfort them and received a nice bite for my trouble. Of course being female I yelled, which made my driver yell that I almost made him wreck the car, thinking my outburst was a "look out!" warning. Finally we got me and all my stuff to the proper ticket check in. He had said he was glad about my condo purchase (glad to see me go?) But when I was ready to get on board and he had walked away he turned and came back saying "What am I doing? I forgot to kiss you". Then he kissed me goodbye. Sometimes it takes a long time to forget.

* * *

"They shall rise up with wings like eagles"
Is 40:31

Chapter 16
CALIFORNIA HERE I COME

My plane taking me to San Diego was nearing landing, coming in over this large lighted city, at 9 o'clock at night. I looked out of the window and thought "Pat you've really done it now; you don't know a soul here!" This city is so large compared to the Chula Vista area where I had bought. I sort of thought that was the whole thing! I didn't really know where I lived now, but I had picked up a hotel lobby brochure in Dallas on the way back from England advising folks to "visit the new Ramada Inn in the heart of the vacationland of San Diego". I checked. Where was Third and Moss? Why it was right in the middle of this vacation land! My son, now in San Francisco, had arranged for his longtime friend from the military to meet me at the airport. He was great, and assured me he knew just where my new address was, ...on the edge of the San Diego country club golf course. God is good. Nancy was obliged to return to L.A. Since her mother was quite ill and her daughter was getting a divorce. She came down to San Diego long enough to teach me how to make a left turn in California traffic and how to dry my stockings rapidly overnight. Since her new boyfriend, who had induced her to move to San Diego was now history, she felt she could do more and better business in LA. We agree she should return there. My son came down at the end of the week to help me hang the hard stuff on the walls and his lovely wife Bonnie came later. She cut the matchstick blinds to fit my windows,- a hard job,- balanced the hanging lamp over the dining room table, and so forth. My son arranged screws in my first floor windows so that they could still slide open but only enough to let in the air; not the burglars.. He also affixed them so that they could not be lifted out, which was easy to do. Then he arranged a lamp to light up the living room and the bedroom if any prowlers came onto my front patio. He was an angel. They were both angels. Then they were off to their respective jobs. I had been worried about my ability to transfer some bearer bonds safely in my book bag. Richard, my son, said I should mail them to him, secured of course. and that he would bring them down when he arrived. But he must've had a change of plans. My bonds arrived by armed guards in uniform! My new neighbors were all assembled to watch me move in and admiring my white bedroom furniture and checking it out. Fortunately I had arranged for a bank and a safe deposit box by long distance before I left Indiana, so the next morning I was able to take the bonds safely to my new bank.

A photo of my new California Condo

* * *

Chapter 17
GETTING SETTLED

The movers placed my furniture but I had lots of boxes to unpack. From one box there jumped ...or was it flew?... a large red cockroach, a Palmetto bug, which gave me quite a start. Fortunately I found a broom and took out after it but it jumped all over the place. The truck which brought my things must have originated in Florida and brought me this little extra surprise. Finally I got settled and found myself sitting in my TV chair watching TV, all alone and wondering what my future would hold. So, out of habit I called up my ex-. I said "Joe, I'm all alone" and he said "where is that other friend of yours from high school, Gloria? Didn't we visit her out there when we took the kids to Disneyland?" Yes, we had visited her in LA but the last postcard I received from her was from France. "I'm sure she's not here" I responded, "that was L.A." He said "it wouldn't hurt to look in the phone book," so I got out the phone book and looked for Gloria. In spite of a name change (she dropped her married name), I found her. She was the third one I called. She was living on Third avenue, about five blocks down the road from me! She was thrilled to hear from me and invited me to her mobile home park and into her impressive swimming pool and hot tub. She introduced me to all sorts of people and organizations. I found San Diego to be open and friendly, perhaps because many, due to the Navy's presence here, had come with the military and stayed, leaving extended family behind. Also many adventurous folk like myself from the Midwest came and stayed. They were mostly all glad to meet new people.

Among others I met Mary who was always ready to go, ..up and at'em, she was 60 going on 40.! I was over 50. She took me to the Chula Vista Public library where an episode of "table tipping" was to be presented, a "mind over matter" demonstration. I figured if sponsored by the public library it must be okay. About five people sat on the stage and held hands. Through mutual concentration they were able to make a card table do all sorts of things, from rotating, to dancing, and bouncing all over the stage! I couldn't believe my eyes. We were invited to come up and examine the chairs and the table. Several of us did that and there was absolutely no wire, string, or any other devise under the plain card table. Then the five invited us to ask questions, stating that the table would answer... one dip for yes; two dips for no. We asked, and the table performed. I thought "what an introduction to California!" I always knew it was different. When I told my number three son about this on the telephone he wisely said, "well mother I guess I won't have to worry about your being lonely out there as long as you have tables to talk to!".

* * *

Chapter 18
THE WONDERS CONTINUE

My new friends took me to many places to acquaint me with the wonders of San Diego.

The greenhouse restaurant, at the 407 and Hwy 8 broadcast live every afternoon. They featured a young blond lady psychic. There was a bandstand, a dance floor and lots of tables and seating. She asked who would like to be "read". I raised my hand. When called upon, I walked to the microphone in the middle of the dance floor. She asked my name. Then she told me I was from a city in the Midwest where I found living like being in a Volkswagen with my fur coat on. (No elbow room) and "You are here to find a partner, possibly two, one for your new career and another for your husband. These two might be the same person." Exactly right! Exactly. Wasn't it odd that my introduction to San Diego included, early on, these two psychic events?

Later on my St. Louis friend who had done so much for me when I had broken my feet, called to see if I had found the woman she had referred me to "just so I would know somebody". This woman had rented to her and her husband when they were first married and helped with the baby before they left for a job in Missouri. I was able to tell her "YES, she was working next door as a housekeeper and secretary! Like finding Gloria so close, and this Josephine too, it just must have been providential. Someone up there likes me.

But it wasn't all good news. One of my experiences in Chula Vista was having my purse snatched when coming out of a Rexall drugstore at 10 PM with my much coveted and hard to come by antibiotics for my Christmas time sore throat. I screamed "oh no, my medicine is in there... you can't have it... my medicine!". .Then the strap broke and he got my purse, but a woman driving by turned into the drive and ran him up against the brick wall! She said" when I saw him struggling with you it made me so mad I forgot I was in my car." He was caught by a store operator at the end of the mall and the police came. I got my purse and my medicine back. He had thrown it under a car. I learned, don't take your purse shopping at night. Wear a belly bag, or better, keep your wallet in an inside pocket.

* * *

Chapter 19
ALL ROADS LEAD TO TIJUANA

Mastering California freeways was not an easy task. Returning to Chula Vista one day to my new home I headed south on "the 405" as they say. I found myself suddenly nearing my exit with five lanes of traffic to cross on my right.. . I did not want to get lost! I knew only one or two routes! My stomach tightened. Perspiration ran down my forehead and into my eye, further obscuring my vision. Shall I chance it? Oh lord what shall I do? All of a sudden my grandfather's voice spoke to me clearly. It said "steady as you go, Pat". I FELT him as well as heard him, and suddenly I felt peaceful. I. got the message. Relax. Slow down. Don't change lanes. You CAN'T GET LOST because all roads lead to Tijuana., which was just 8 miles down the road from my garden apartment condo. Yes the two main southbound highways, the 5 and the 405 came together at Tijuana. My heart beat wildly when I saw in my side mirror, pulling up from riding in my blind spot, a motorcyclist. Had I swung toward my exit, I would've killed him.

* * *

"Hang in there baby"

Chapter 20
LICENSING PROBLEMS

A year passed. Time to go to work! Due to the 1982 recession jobs were scarce. No one was hiring. The County was not hiring,- in fact the County was laying off. I decided to go into private practice which my degree permitted. I joined a group in a big old house downtown where I could schedule clients along with other therapists using the same offices. There would be someone to answer the phone. I joined the Private Practice society and attended meetings in order to become known and hopefully get referrals. Meanwhile I learned that Family and Children's Association in Escondido was offering space and referrals on a self-employed basis, with pay for clients seen and no percs. I applied and went to work there- working part-time for almost 3 years, barely getting by. The training and supervision were good and I met fine colleagues (one allowed me to stay nearby occasionally at her beautiful home with guest house and swimming pool, so I wouldn't have to travel back and forth so far.) I worked from 1 to 9 pm and the commute from my home was 33 miles each way often returning home through dense fog. Very dangerous. Plus I worked part time in Poway, a branch office about 10 miles nearer. I worked alone there. The office was at one end of a strip mall. Stores were closed in the evening except the liquor store at the other end. I started wearing an alarm on my wrist which, when you pushed the button, emitted a loud fog horn blast. I also stopped booking any male clients after five o'clock. When I left there at nine or 10 PM I made a run for my car while praying a lot. I had heard of a social worker in Santa Monica who was murdered by one of her clients.

I had enrolled for the extra classes required by the State of California and was ready to take the exam. But the Powers That Be in Sacramento - the state capital - said "oh no you must have three more years of supervised experience under a California clinical social worker before you can take the exam!" I blew my top. "How, I asked, can I be expected to do that when it is not possible to get a job just now? If I don't go into private practice then I will just starve!. Is that what you want?" Well – they reconsidered. After all, some therapists move with their husband's careers and they need to be licensed anywhere.

They advised me to get a complete background history of my supervising psychiatrist and my supervising social worker back in Fort Wayne Indiana, and that was to include their education as well as their total experience. I felt bad . How could I ask them to do that? But I asked them, and they came through with it all, willingly, 'happy to help me' and with best wishes for my future. And so I took the exams up at Long Beach in L.A, about 125 miles up the coast.. A new friend loaned me her friend for driving,– and that was great even though he warned me he had a tendency to fall asleep at the wheel! Narcolepsy? I was as yet unaccustomed to driving the CA. freeways so it was a matter of deciding who was the more dangerous driver,.. him or me. I decided to take a chance on him! The exams went well and I bought lunch for us at Marie Callendar's, a restaurant overlooking a beautiful lagoon with yachts in port. What a view!, especially for me, being from the land-locked Midwest. When we started back my helper said "I'll drive first" and he did... until he fell asleep in the fast lane. With us heading for the divider wall I grabbed the wheel and miraculously got us over to the right shoulder, crossing 5 lanes to our off ramp. I drove the rest of the way and it was hard, with the fast-moving weekend traffic from L.A. to San Diego, and me with little California driving experience.

* * *

Chapter 21
MY PROFESSIONAL DREAM IS FULFILLED

While I was waiting for my licensing, I worked at Family and Children's service. Commuting was hard on those fast-moving highways but it was worth it. Sometimes while pondering cases, or being obstructed by a large truck, I would miss my exit. No problem. I just went on to San Marcos and doubled back when I could find an exit. (Sometimes that exit was a long way down the road!)

In school I had learned how to help depressed persons and those with anxiety disorders. Depressed housewives were my specialty. (I had first-hand knowledge of these!) My colleagues thought I was good, as we co-led groups, or by hearing me through the wall next door as I worked with individuals. They were nice enough to tell the supervisor at the staff meeting which put me at ease. In fact it brought tears to my eyes. I had also been trained in helping failing marriages which was especially rewarding for me. It was easier to be a specialist than a generalist in my opinion. My favorite subject was Communications, which involved learning to identify the feelings of other persons and respond in a supportive way in order that they can see that you understand; as well as to learn to identify and express one's own feelings in a nonthreatening way. Assertiveness training and the use of non-threatening "I feel" messages (which did not make the other feel attacked) were much in style at that time. 'I did family therapy where everyone's needs and opinions are heard and respected. It was exciting to me to be able to share ways in which we could all be happier and to observe people as they came up with their own solutions which fit them.

In my parenting groups, I taught parents how to use choices and rewards effectively when dealing with their children. Let them choose, and look at the probable consequences with them. Ask "what will you do then; how will that work for you". It really beats yelling and punishing and spares the yeller (that's usually mom) from feeling like a monster. Given a choice children feel empowered and become more cooperative. After all, it's their choice, arrived at by exploring consequences rather than being demanded by parents. A once-a-week family round-table at home gave every family member a voice,- a chance to be heard and acknowledged.

As I tried, I learned how I should have raised my own, had I known. Too late? No. They turned out well and I shared my life-changing knowledge with them, when appropriate, as adults. After all, they would be raising children too.

* * *

Chapter 22
WONDERFUL SAN DIEGO

So life proceeded. My sister came to visit and marveled at the weather and the palm trees. We visited Old Town and ate at the Casa de Bandidi restaurant sitting under colorful Spanish umbrellas next to a bubbling fountain. My friend Gloria and I had taken up Spanish at night school. I practiced it on the waiters, much to my sister's surprise. We visited the beautifully tiled old Globe theater with its gorgeous Mid Eastern dome rising high, then the gardens and the museums. Although impressed, she was not amenable to moving. She liked the green of Missouri. Gloria introduced me to lots of people and clubs and organizations. We were invited to join a group traveling to Tijuana for a fashion show and lunch at the Tijuana country club. It was great to try the authentic food (especially a dessert called flan), and then see the beautiful models on the runway. This was followed by a tour of the homes and neighborhoods., from grand and gorgeous to not so grand. At home again the phone rang and we were invited to a day at a ranch, owned by one of the museum's docents. (We had signed up as museum volunteers). It was a fun day and I marveled at the friendliness and openness of the San Diego people.

My sister having returned home, my friend introduced me to the leader of the Women's club. She had been a drama major in college and was now a producer of plays for the ladies' societies. I was given a leading part and had my picture in the "social doings" column in the newspaper! Then she told me I must go for bridge lessons because bridge was an important part of the local social doings. I did as instructed found her to be correct, since almost all groups and organizations had a supplementary bridge chapter. Fortunately I had learned beginning bridge in St. Louis some years ago, although my husband and I had played only briefly.

I was invited to join a choir, a women's chorus, the Masonic Lodge, and the Thursday club, which met at the Chula Vista golf course club house. This was a charming place with Spanish architecture, and with arched windows looking out on rose gardens and the golf course. There was a luncheon. There was a stage. There was entertainment with every meeting. I marveled at the lifestyle here. Back home there had been only church and the garden club, and the Community Players, at least in my neighborhood. Daytime entertainment, never. Why is there so much talent here I wondered? Well talent was drawn to California in the 20s and 30s, the early days of moving picture making. According to my grandmother, my mother, who produced a show at the local Congregational Church at age 16 was deemed to have talent and was invited by a scout to come to Hollywood; which she did not do. I suppose many who came West hoping for a career in pictures stayed, successful or not, because of the weather – – and their children and grandchildren are here. Musicians found work here and, in L.A., at the movie studios.

When I joined the volunteers at the Museum of Natural History I met a friend who played piano and organ. She and I and several others entertained in the museum and at the mall at Balboa Park for Christmas, Cinco de Mayo, and other special days. Another group I joined met for dinner and theater at the Old Globe once a month. We were included in Las Vegas night, (a political fund raiser), and helped with ushering in the open air Starlight Theater whenever they were short handed. We participated in the opening of a new shopping center by staffing the "painting machines" for the children. This women's group was often called whenever an event needed reliable persons to help, which opened interesting activity to me, activity that I would never have imaged. One year I was a Santa-costumed bell ringer in front of the grocery store, for the Salvation Army! I was also a happy singer in a trio at the Church of Religious Science for a while. The preacher and his wife, also a preacher, had been well known child movie stars!. It was for me a wonderful and amazing time.

* * *

Chapter 23
ANOTHER PREDICTIVE DREAM

I was sitting in a gorgous home with beautiful people on a California mountain side participating in an Edgar Cayce (the Sleeping Prophet) Search for God group. I admitted to feeling a little inferior and a little sorry for myself that I had to conserve dollars so carefully. I had only a part-time job and had to commute 33 miles each way. Gas had gone to $1.50 per gallon! and might go higher. People waited in line to fill up. (This was 1983.) I looked at my blue plastic purse and vowed, "someday I'll get a real leather one". (Sounds ridiculous now). With my education I had done my part in getting ready for prosperity. Whatever brought on these self-pitying feelings, that night I dreamed of my grandmother's gold watch. It was a strong dream. It seemed to say to me "money, or valuables from the family, are coming to you." Or something like that. I told the members of the group about my dream in order to document it in case this dream came true. I also wrote a note about it in the inside cover of my "Search for God" textbook.(I still have the book), Meanwhile I got a high paying job in Hemet, Ca. Which literally saved my financial life. The job jacked up my Social Security times three, and gave me a pension in only six years of employment. Then, in the mid 1990's my second cousin died. She was my grandmother's niece, leaving my sisters and me a surprise inheritance. Not a really big one but more than we had imagined and it gave me everything that I needed. My cousin had never married, and had no siblings or children. She had a modest job as a book keeper, and later a credit officer. A life time job. The money came from my great-grandfather's new-to-St. Louis telephone company, Kusel Electric Co. which I had only vaguely heard of. I believe there was a family falling out and the money went to my grandmother's sister... who cared for the parents until their death. Thank goodness this inheritance finally made it to the right person,... me! So the dream came true which had been telling me, "don't worry; everything is going to change for the better.!"

* * *

Chapter 24
I MOVE AGAIN

Between the distance, danger, and the inadequate income of my job I wanted to find something better. On Sundays I watched a famous female West Coast preacher, Terry Cole Whitaker, who broadcast from the El Cortez Hotel in downtown San Diego. She preached positive thinking, making positive affirmations, and she preached prosperity. "Give and you'll receive" was her concept (keep it moving), a concept shared by Hans Selye who gave us the "give to get" syndrome, a concept also given by Jesus who said "cast thy bread upon the water and it will return to you". (From the Loaves and Fishes sermon on the Mount). In other words, share and there will be enough for all. Ms. Whitaker taught making affirmations, that is " name it and claim it!". (Ask and you shall receive? That's biblical too.) I thought it worth trying. After all, what was there to lose? My budget was tight and I had my retirement to think of. So I tried it. I affixed a large sign on the inside of my front door saying "I claim $50,000." I GOT IT.! This is how. I began reading the monthly social work news. Hemet, San Bernardino, and Palm Springs were all advertising for therapists! It seemed there were too many in San Diego, the very desirable place to live, and these places further up the line were short and paying almost 3 times what I was presently making,.. since I was working for a charitable institution supported by United Way. I made a few interview trips, applied, and they hired me in Hemet, which was in Riverside County. It was 90 miles up the road and I had three weeks to get there, and first I had to squeeze in a trip to Hawaii that I had promised my #3 son, his having been given tickets by my #1 son. I bought a rental contract, a book of receipts, and advertised my condo for rent. (This was okay with the management.) I made another trip to Hemet to search for a rental for myself. A real estate company helped and I found an adorable freestanding cottage/condo with great neighbors across the walkway. The rent was a little less than I was asking for my San Diego condo. I had just unpacked my back bedroom and squared everything away, since it was my turn to host three tables of bridge in San Diego. Now I had to pack it all up again. Upon return from our trip to Hawaii I found a suitable tenant, called the moving company, and would you believe it my tenants were moving in the same day I was moving out! It was a bit crowded, but possible. Now in Hemet I lived six blocks from the clinic where I was newly employed and had no trucks to dodge. It was worth it, the move that is, and this town was charming, surrounded by snow-capped mountains (at least in Feb), and surrounded also by turkey farms, goat farms, horses and cattle. Access to Riverside was through a lovely picturesque canyon with curving narrow roads. Then you came out on Hwy 10, which also took you to Palm Springs, depending on which way you turned. I started working with adults, with unusual problems, personal and marital, but after two years that division was closed, on account of budget cutbacks, and I was transferred to the chronic cases. I was really getting a thorough training. The last two years of the six years I stayed I spent working with children, parents, and schools. These Riverside schools were great in that they referred any children with behavior problems or failing grades to the Mental Health Center. I did a lot of family therapy.

My first supervisor was a woman psychologist who drove us to Palm Springs for off-season or end of season shopping. We were able to buy high style quality clothes deeply discounted at high end stores and also at resell-it shops, where the rich frequently placed their clothing having worn them only once! And of course Palm Springs was a divine place with divine restaurants, some with giant carp fish ponds on either side of the entrance. The mountains, when coming in over Highway 10 through the desert were lovely. The same supervisor owned a sailing boat and offered to take us sailing on Lake Perris, although I personally never got the chance to go. Alas, after two years she went into private practice and left us.

Right there next to Hemet, up a winding road to a mountain top, lay Idlewild, a community with A-frame houses, vacation homes, gift shops and restaurants. I had joined Parents without Partners and another member, a school teacher, had us to her home up there for a meeting. I was impressed. I had been told that Idlewild was the home of a boy's school which was attended by Frank Sinatra's son. That fact (and the gorgeous tall pine trees), attracted tourists,- at least out-of-state people like myself. When looking over the back side of the mountain, far below, you could see Palm Springs. I was privileged to visit this spot several time with friends but could never get up the nerve to drive that steep, cliff side road for myself. For one thing my car's motor had seen better days; and my friend and colleague's son had ended up with his little red truck hanging halfway on and halfway off the cliff at a curve! We were glad to be able to report that he survived.

My salary rose quite a bit every year, and along with a few private clients on evenings and the weekend, I was able to save $20,000 a year! In five years I had twice the amount of money I had 'claimed', plus a new Oldsmobile. I believe had it not been for the lecture of Ms. Whitaker's and the 'Claim It' sign I put up, which raised my awareness, I would probably have discarded the social work newsletter without really reading it or even considered making such a change. Her teaching made me believe that it was possible, so I went for it! In 6 years I was now over 60, and ready to retire. I received my pension, promised all my friends and co-workers to visit, and returned to beautiful San Diego.

* * *

"They that sow in tears shall reap in joy"
Psalms 126

Chapter 25
DREAMS DO COME TRUE

When I was considering my new professional career, and often plagued with doubt, my #1 son sent me a small concrete castle made to look like a sand castle. Topped with a flag, the message was "dreams DO come true." That was so like him to care and send me a little `upper.' I guess the sand castle was right because my dreams were coming true, my return to California being one of them. I had spent a year here when I was 19 years old and had never forgotten it. I had returned to Missouri when World War II ended and I had spent the next 20 years trying to convince the family to try California. Now it happened, however without the family, and the experience turned out to be far more then I could have asked for. My professional work I counted as a success and also my life, because it had changed so much. I had learned much that was interesting as well as useful. I was no longer disgruntled and unhappy. My last wish? How about true love? I hadn't been lucky in love. I had given up dating almost immediately after the divorce when I went with girlfriends to the St. Louis Single's dances and observed middle aged men dancing with the 20-year-olds. I never felt like such a wallflower! I also discovered that expectations had changed since high school dating. I was questioned about my sexual intentions by one date before he would decide to pay for dinner! I decided to devote myself to my new education and career. I decided that "if the Lord wanted me to have a man he would bring him to me" and that is just what happened ... 16 years later.

Chula Vista, a suburb of San Diego had a beautiful million dollars senior center where, upon my return from Hemet, we played bridge. Lessons were at 10 AM. I took a lot of lessons having been advised to do so in order to fit into the local social life. I was coming along pretty well and was now, as my friend Mary stated "ready for the Center". In time a new partner sat down with me and gave me a few pointers. It was Larry, my true love to be. He had beautiful blue eyes, a clear suntanned skin, and wavy white hair. Since he walked a lot, he was able to keep his weight right. My new girlfriend Mary and I always drove him home. Although he walked to the Center he appreciated a ride home. We stopped for coffee and pie. It wasn't long till my girl friend said, "I feel like an unneeded third-party. You two just can't take your eyes off each other". I was thrilled to discover that he liked opera (he was part Italian) and the ballet, stage plays and symphonies! He loved hearing our ladies' barbershop harmony group sing at patio parties, especially the way we could break right into harmony acappella just amazed him.

This is my Dreams Come True Sandcastle.

It looked like our vibes matched in other ways too. He was a retired accountant and could balance a checkbook! When I was named Treasurer of the National Women's Organization he helped me with the books, showing me how to record entries in order to leave a paper trail for auditing. And he liked Church! – a first in my relationships.

We refinished furniture together without any mutual aggravation,- another first,- and, we ate out every evening since "he didn't like doing dishes, which was only fair if I cooked" he said. We went to bridge parties and hostessed bridge parties and potlucks. We had a great group of friends. On holidays we were never left home alone.

We traveled to Alaska, to Europe, and to the Eastern Mediterranean countries newly out from under the Soviet occupation. We loved Venice and Constantinople. Talk about a dream boat, we had seven lovely years together. Unfortunately Larry smoked, chain style, and otherwise than a couple of burns on my car roof and floor, it wasn't a problem since he agreed to do it outside. But I worried about his health. I took him on 10 consecutive Saturday mornings to a "stop smoking class" and he cut down from almost 3 packs per day, to one.

Larry kept the doctor checking for lung cancer but it was emphysema that did him in. When we visited the Museums in Balboa Park he would have to stop every few yards to get his breath. Once I had to push him up a small hill! I felt I needed to return to my roots where I had two sons and my only grandchild, and I felt it better not to wait until Larry's health got worse. I had meant to return to St. Louis as soon as I retired, but then I found Larry and we both loved San Diego. We had wonderful times together in California but it seemed that now was the time to go home. We decided to keep his small apartment in Chula Vista and buy a house in St Louis. Then we could be "snow birds" who spent winters in the warmest place, California! I remember telling our bridge leader the year before that we might be leaving soon. I showed him a photo of the lovely white snow in my son's new front yard and my granddaughter making a snowman. He asked "when do you plan to go?" I said "oh in a year or two". He said, "By that time maybe you'll come to your senses!" But, now was the time. Larry couldn't do much to help with the move besides sit and mark the boxes' destinations with a black marker... kitchen, bedroom, etc. We hated to leave but I knew the end was growing near for him, and I needed to be nearer to my family. We found a house, made the move, found a bridge group and I found a chorus to sing in,- the Sweet Adelines. He died four months after we arrived.

* * *

Chapter 26
THE INCONVENIENT GRANDMOTHER

Homecoming was a disappointment. I had been warned by friends in San Diego who had returned to their roots, that although they lived "next door" they "never saw them". Family members had built their lives around their work, other events, and other people. And they were busy... as everyone is these days. I had wanted to go to Florida to live but my son and daughter-in-law were both professional people whose jobs required a great deal of travel. My son didn't feel comfortable about my being there alone as I grew older, when they were gone so much. Besides my one and only grandchild was now eight years old and growing up fast in St. Louis, so I had decided that we should go there. Jennifer, my St. Louis daughter-in-law, worked full time plus caring for the home and a child, and had two aging parents who were in and out of the hospital, and needed her attention. My son David worked two jobs, one being his beloved band job which played weekends at the nearby Holiday Inn, with practice sessions on some weeknights too. They just didn't have "five minutes of time" or so my Florida son explained. I found myself left out of most social events with them and their friends and this included vacations. They went to her extended family for holidays although they found a spot for my third son Paul and me to celebrate holidays at another time. My third son Paul worked nights and of course recreated with his friends on most weekends. I missed my friends in California... I missed the beach and the good weather and outdoor events such as Walking Club and patio potlucks. Not surprisingly, with Larry gone and most every thing else, I got depressed. My Florida son called and offered to help me move back to San Diego, but alas my condo, which I had had a hard time selling three years previously was now caught in the real estate bubble and worth four times what I had sold it for! I couldn't afford to buy there now!

* * *

Chapter 27
WE JOIN THE GLITTERATTI

Then Rich and Bonnie began providing me with exciting events to look forward to, and so it worked out both ways.

First, there were frequent visits to their fabulous Florida home, on the Bay, with a fun swim pool off the living room terrace and a small cruiser at the dock. There was the beach, great little restaurants featuring crab cakes and seafood, (my favorites), and visits with her parents, – loving, warm and friendly as any parents could be, definitely my type. We loved swapping stories and had a lot of laughs. They asked me to join them on cruises and trips. My number three son shared my cabin on Caribbean cruises on two consecutive Thanksgivings, and then later on, a Christmas in Hawaii. Rich's wife Bonnie, being an executive was occasionally given tickets for various upscale events, usually amazing to me. We attended the Tony awards in New York, a high-fashion black-tie event, where we met and had our photos taken with Karen Zambia, a 2001 Tony award winner, up on top of the RCA building in the Rainbow Room during the preshow cocktail hour. Later, we spied Betty Garrett outside the stage door signing autographs. Following the cocktail hour we found our seats in the huge Radio City auditorium, with everyone chattering expectantly. Then the lights began to dim, the chattering ceased, and the announcer's voice warned us..,"three, two, one,.. WE'RE ON THE AIR". There was a hush, and then full applause broke out as the television cameras took over and the show began. It was of course a wonderful show, with Mel Brooks winning most of the awards for The Producers. At the end, everyone stood up. Was there a press toward the exits? Oh no! We all stood and gazed at each other, main floor and balcony, at the women's beautiful gowns and the handsome tuxedoed men. A celebrity packed dinner followed the show, at the Sheraton Hotel two blocks away. That walk made ME feel like a celebrity with the interested New Yorkers cheering us from behind the yellow crowd-containing ribbons. We were served cocktails along the way! "Now it looks" my son said to me "like WE are the glitteratti!" It was an amazing feeling, although it was of course untrue. I would think that those behind the yellow ribbon would feel jealous or resentful but they did not,... they only cheered. Apparently they loved just being close to the:glitteratti". Mel Brook's play was the funniest play I have never seen. (I say never because I had to wait for the movie, and it was funny!) At the banquet we were at the next table to celebrities such as Jean Smart of TV fame's Designing Women, and Henry Winkler, the Fonzie, and among other guests we were privileged to see were Michelle Lee, Anne Bancroft and Glenn close. The table décor, as well as the food were fabulous and I was, once more impressed, - and amazed at my good luck of being there.

April of 2003 brought Bonnie tickets to the Easter Egg Roll on the White House lawn. We took along my granddaughter, now 12 years old, for the history so prominently displayed in Washington DC and of course to see the White House interior too. The biggest surprise for her were the soldiers doing exercises and formations on the lawn in front of the Marble Memorials! I don't think she had ever seen a real soldier before. Then we were treated to a welcoming talk by Lynne Cheney (Mrs. VP). My son got a lucky photo shot of her and Kristen and me shaking hands and then we had breakfast at the White House!

WE JOIN THE GLITTERATTI

These are of the White House Egg Roll and breakfast.

At another time there was a trip to New York to see the Broadway musical 42nd St. Our seats were just seven rows back and on the aisle. I had never been treated to such luxury, and LOVED the show. We visited a fancy New York restaurant after the show for a late supper, "just like the rich people do!" The next morning we rode a horse and carriage through Central Park and ate genuine New York cheesecake at Lindy's. And best of all they took me to Paris on the occasion of Rich's 50th birthday. We walked from the Arch d'Triump down to the Sacré Coeur Cathedral, at which point my feet hurt so much I could not get up the long stairs to see inside the church! Fortunately a sightseeing tram was passing and we hailed it, and so went on to Mont Martre viewing, - sitting down!

Richard bought an experimental small airplane and flew to St. Louis now and then. It lacked all- weather landing equipment so once on his way to an air show in Wisconsin he became weathered-in at St. Louis for five days. I was glad for the visit and praying the weather wouldn't clear up too soon! We ended by seeing part of that show on TV on the Speed Channel, to my surprise, then finally he was able to take off and see the rest of the show in Wisconsin. I was not fond however of the airplane, a tiny two-seater, – but he assured me it was safe and being an experienced Naval pilot, new what he was doing. He always checked the preflight checklist carefully as well as keeping up the maintenance. I couldn't even get into this tiny plane on account of my 20+ pounds (probably too much cheesecake). In time Rich and Bonnie acquired a four seater, a 2 engine Barron. Now they could fly family members to different states to visit each other, fly Mom and Dad to their cruises' Ports of Embarkation, and to see their daughter's family in Georgia. This plane had an instrument panel for landing in the fog, so I couldn't expect him to be trapped in St. Louis any more!.

WE JOIN THE GLITTERATTI

This is Richard's new airplane the Baron.

* * *

Chapter 28
WE FLY TO KEY WEST

The forecast wasn't perfect, but the day was so sunny we decided to take a trip by plane, my first with pilot Richard. It was Labor Day 2002. We flew along the East Coast over the inland waterways. What a view! The sky was so blue and little white clouds floated by. My ears predictably protested at 7000 feet, so we lowered our altitude a bit. Bonnie and I were all done up in our ear phones so we could communicate with the pilot. However we were asked to keep that to necessities like watching for and reporting small planes on either side of us. Landing was a hoot, watching from the back seat over the pilot's shoulder as the ground came up closer and closer... and there, – we're down. That was a first for me and I marveled at my son's skill and professionalism talking to the tower at both take off and landing and of course, his skills in flying the plane and knowing what all that dashboard instrumentation meant. We had lunch, looked at Ernest Hemingway attractions, watched the boats come and go and had an enjoyable time, although it was hot.! I felt I may have sweated off 10 pounds although my scale, later on, did not agree. Halfway home the little white clouds became the thick black clouds, hemming us in. Richard reassured us that there were many small landing fields all over Florida where we could put down at any time. Bonnie said she was just about ready for that, -landing, that is. She said she had always been a "white knuckle flier", strange for someone whose job kept her in the air a good deal of the time! I was impressed with the fact that the "ground" as they call it knew just where we were and what the conditions were. We hadn't filed a flight plan, and yet they knew we were up there, God bless 'em. They directed us to an opening to the West as we were heading for St. Petersburg on the West coast, but by the time we reached the opening it had closed. So they redirected us northeast to Tampa and there we made a safe landing. We enjoyed a great steak in a Tampa restaurant, rented a car, and took off for home,- leaving the plane at the Tampa airport. The next morning Rich drove up there, turned in the car, collected the Barren and flew it home. What an adventure! It was beginning to look like my Golden years were going to be golden after all.

WE FLY TO KEY WEST

In November of 2005 I was invited again to New York where Rich and Bonnie had a charming small apartment high up in a skyscraper in Manhattan just next door to Carnegie Hall. Bonnie was doing some temporary work from there and also doing a speaking tour. Rich seemed to bend over backward to see that I saw all the spots and got to do all of the things I had in memory from when I lived and worked there for a year when I was 20. (My sister and I had been transferred there by Western Union Telegraph Co., our very first jobs out of high school, as they needed extra help during the war.) Richard and I rode the subway for old times sake and he thanked me for some high points he remembered when he was growing up, and for my efforts as a mother. This was really not like him, except for compliments and thank yous on birthday cards. He asked me questions about family matters (the divorce) that he had never asked before. I wondered. Otherwise than that, he was particularly pleased with my having lost 23 pounds, both for my improved appearance and for my health, since he knew I was in the "metabolic syndrome" which is prediabetes. The next morning Rich and Bonnie had to leave early to meet a client for a game of golf in New Jersey, so I called a limousine myself and made it to the airport on my own.

The flight was prolonged on account of storms around Houston and we were routed out over the Gulf of Mexico and back again through San Antonio. My flight connection to St. Louis,- the last one for the night, should have gone, but happily they waited for us. Upon arrival I retrieved my car from the airport lot and drove the "speedway" home, arriving at 11:30 PM instead of 9 PM, still alert and awake. I didn't mind. I had had such a sweet and lovely time with Richard and Bonnie, their being so attentive and eager to please.

* * *

Chapter 29
CHRISTMAS IN HAWAII

In December, both families, Richard's and Bonnie's, flew to Hawaii for Christmas. Richard was especially glad to have his brother David and family since they had not been able to participate in the other cruises due to work conflicts and financial limitations. Family expenses, included braces for my granddaughter's teeth, and of course adding any spare dollars to her college fund. They did visit at Rich and Bonnie's home in Florida. Rich and his brother David had been close growing up. It's nice to have a brother, five years older, who knows how to assemble gocarts and such! So Richard was especially enthusiastic about this forthcoming trip, hoping it would all go well. It did go well. It went well biking down the mountain, a new thrill for Kristen, my granddaughter (and kinda scary!) Then walking to see the volcanoes spewing forth, (walking on that black uneven lava is not easy); then boating through the grottoes, enjoying entertainment aboard. We visited a spot where the steam roared out from below and when the wind changed it suddenly blew right on us, and burned! though not badly. I jumped back quickly and hid my face. The hotel was great, the food was great and walking on the beach was fun. Then, armed with gobs of photos, it was time for the long flight home in time for the New Year.

One thing the new year brought was a jobless Paul, my #3 son. He had lost his job of 12 years when it "went to China", as did his cousin Johnny, who had been on his job for 20 years. Paul was not a good candidate for retraining. As he progressed in high school it appeared that his focus and interest weren't there. We had taken him to a doctor for tests and been advised to let him quit 10th grade and go into factory work. Paul did not like this and insisted on finishing high school, which he did, with a little help from an excellent tutor. I am very proud of him for that, since it preserved his self esteem. However he had always done manufacturing work but now he has been unable to find work for several years, except for low-paying part-time temporary work with no percs and no health insurance. With the current recession, or crisis, he can find nothing, US manufacturing having gone overseas. Ross Perot was right when he said "If NAFTA passes, "there will be a great whistling noise as jobs fly out of this country". This prolonged jobless situation was and is a great worry for both him and me. He wants to work and feels anxious, bored, and useless with no paycheck coming in. Can't anything ever go right? I had thought that he was set until Social Security took over.

And so I felt the need to put Paul's inheritance in trust to be administered by his brother Richard, who flew to St. Louis to help me redo my Will. I depended on him so much. He was my helper and my personal therapist,- always willing to listen and give me support and advice. He called almost every Sunday evening, sometimes from unusual places... as from an airplane or from a foreign country. He always said "Hello mother, this is Richard", in that sweet, pleasant voice of his.

In March of the new year I went to California with a friend to see a California friend. It was good to get away from the dreary winter days of the Midwest. I hadn't heard from Richard for a while. When I called they said he's been flying a lot and meditating, unusual for him. They said he was considering taking a job delivering small planes from the factory to new owners, and sometimes refurbished ones. He retired too early and was wanting something to do in the flying world. Although he did participate in a group which helped and encouraged young would-be fliers, and sat on the board for Continental Express, it was a difficult decision to make. In early May they would fly to New York to meet with the people offering this opportunity and make a trial flight.

* * *

"Nothing is forever"

Chapter 30
BAD NEWS

I had been missing Larry, and missing my beloved blue eyed Siamese cat which was killed on the road near my home while chasing a raccoon off his property. It was amazing how much I grieved for that cat. I thought I would never get over it. He was both beautiful and special, both intelligent and loving. I was feeling lonely. I sat out on my new screened porch on a fine day early in May, watching the sprinkler spew it's sun-sparkled drops across the landscape. I gazed across the back lawns which, because there are no fences, make a lovely grassy lane like a park. Suddenly everything started to glow. What is this I thought, another "alpha" experience? It was like God was raising my consciousness saying: "I am here for you". This had happened to me in San Diego the night before my next door neighbor died. As I left her apartment the sunset was unbelievably gorgeous, more than I have ever seen it in that land of beautiful sunsets. The music coming home from her place sounded heavenly. I asked the housekeeper about the gorgeous music and she said, "oh it's just the radio". The next day I found my neighbor sitting in her chair, the phone ringing insistently at her feet, and she was gone. I felt sad and really spooked, as well as confused. Fortunately my #3 son was visiting me and told me who to call. Later on I looked up "the alpha state". It was defined as "sensing a larger world outside of yourself"... and according to J. Kluger, writer of "The Biology of Belief", published in Time magazine February 23 09, the parietal lobe at the top of the brain is responsible for this. The type of stimulation needed for this to occur was not mentioned.

But back to my screened porch experience in St. Louis. After a while I went to bed. That night I had a powerful dream –... the kind too real, too puzzling to ignore. In the dream I lay in a bunk in the prow of a friend's boat, a boat we had sailed on down at the Lake of the Ozarks. The hatch door to the deck was just inches above my nose. My son Rich was standing on an elevated sidewalk next to the boat and smiling down at me. A woman walked on the same sidewalk, about 30 or 40 feet behind. Another followed looking neat and petite and maybe 40 years old. Just nice, serious appearing people going on about their business in a fresh place,– -but where? The world and its ugliness was down in the hold of the cruiser signified by dirt, trash, and disorder. "I want to go UP." I want to go UP", but I couldn't quite make it. I was close, but not quite close enough. The following day the dream stuck with me. "What" I asked myself "did I want to go up TO"? Rich and Bonnie's social class? Their financial status? I was mystified,- for the time being.

* * *

Chapter 31
WORSE NEWS

On the ninth of May I got sick, out of the blue. I hadn't felt bad at all that day. But now I felt sick Big Time, and around 5 pm I called my #2 son who lived nearby. He came over and sat with me and had to bring me the bucket. I was that sick...and for no reason I could pinpoint. After an hour or so I felt better and he went home. I believe now it was a premonition of what was to come.

The next morning I felt fairly okay but took a nap at 2:30 PM. At about 3 PM I was awakened by an airplane engine SO loud and so low, in the sky just over my garage. WHAT IS THAT? I hope it doesn't hit my house! I wanted to get up and see, but I was so tired... The roaring stopped, abruptly. That's strange I thought. Planes don't just stop in mid-air...they taper off as they distance themselves. I fell back asleep for a little while, then woke suddenly and stood up. It was 3:30 PM "straight up and down", exactly. "Oh, I thought it was later than that". I felt a little discombobulated. Everything `felt` so quiet. Then, in a few hours, the phone rang. It was Bonnie's mother from Florida. She said " how are you?" I said "well I think the flu..." "Pat", she said "I have something bad to tell you. Something very bad.... Richard has been killed in a plane accident". Richard? Where? How? I could barely speak. She must mean someone else. Her husband had been quite ill, being treated for cancer actually. She must've meant Irving. Rich and Bonnie were in New York. They had been buying me a birthday gift and ordering flowers for Mother's Day. But as it turned out, Rich and Bonnie had parted in New York.

She flew home to Florida and he was flying to Las Vegas with the person who had told him about the plane ferrying job. The plane they flew was not new, and it was experimental. It had been in the shop in Pennsylvania having the upholstery repaired. This pilot said that he personally owned one just like it and that these planes were safe. They were careful to do the total checklist before taking off and the routine maintenance, always. Rich's friends said that he was a careful pilot. Having done that, they took off. They rose 100 feet above the airfield and the engine failed. Facing a school and homes near the end of the runway, they could not glide to a landing. They had to turn sharply back to the field. The steep turn put them into a tailspin from which they could not recover, and- both men died.

Plans were made for all of us to fly to Florida. The accident occurred in Pennsylvania and it took several days to release the body. Bonnie had not even known of the crash. She had not been contacted until a helper at the hangar gave her the news. Fortunately Bonnie had many friends,- among them a female in the undertaking business. She went to Pennsylvania to check and see why they were holding him and to mend the body as best she could. She did a good job, an amazing job. When we arrived at the funeral home and crematorium, on my birthday May 15, we beheld our beloved brother, uncle, and son lying on a gurney partially covered with a blanket, his face quite swollen, with two small cuts that had been stitched, and beneath the blanket, broken bones. I could see it was him – – his beautiful profile and hairline and hands just like my fathers. I kissed his cheek and his temple, held his hands and tried not to die from grief. I sat by his side quietly for a long long time, until they came to take him to the crematorium.

Pennsylvania is northeast of St. Louis, and my garage is just on the northeast side of my house. That final roar came to me from a long way away, just as the shot had done when my father died.

* * *

Chapter 32
THE FUNERAL

The funeral took place in Rich's double airplane hangar, with large photo boards and a revolving video of special life events that he and Bonnie had shared. His large white motorcycle, without a rider, and the small plane, without a pilot, stood at the hangers end.. A lovely display of flowers was all about and there were musicians.

It was well attended. The multiple eulogies described my son as an honest, kind, and talented man, – – generous and helpful, beloved by his nieces and brothers, his colleagues and friends. There was music and the vocalist sang his favorite songs, such as "Blue skies, smiling at me". A female Navy chaplain gave an inspiring talk. The Navy sent a pair of cadets to do their honor routine along with the folding and presentation of the flag to the widow. At the end there was a flyover, low over the hangar with the pilot's dipping the wings to say goodbye, as Richard had always done when taking off and leaving us. This was the most touching event. It was followed by a reception at the house, with caterers taking over the dining room and beverages being served outside around the pool. The glass sliding doors which line the long living room had been removed to allow easy access to the pool area. Tall flower arrangements adorned the living room and hall, sent by colleagues and well-wishers.

Afterwards we were very tired. We stayed another day, sat out on the dock, and mentally said goodbye to all that beauty and all of these things which reminded us of him, including the ship, now without a captain. His brother broke down at that point and had a good cry. Then we caught a plane to St. Louis.

* * *

Chapter 33
I'VE HAD ENOUGH

Five days after the funeral I sat on my lounge on the deck on a lovely May morning. I thought, "I don't understand God. He's supposed to be merciful and understanding. Why did he allow this, - the very WORST thing that could possibly have happened to me?" No I don't understand Him and I've HAD ENOUGH. David and Jennifer will probably be relieved not to have my old age on their hands. And Paul really needs my money, such as it is, more than he needs me. Yes I've had enough. I'm not afraid anymore." I had a wide hose in the garage to attach to the car muffler. I could put the seat back in a reclining position and end my anguish for ever.... I started to get up – when,... ALL of a sudden there was a burst of energy and light, shaped like a rocket, evanescent like champaign, erupting next to and above my lounge!

It was accompanied by the MOST ECSTATIC FEELINGS of joy, I have ever known. It was `school picnic morning AND I won the lottery' and much more. Then a familiar voice said "Mom, wait'll you see this!" It was Richard,.. followed by "You'll be comfortable there for the time you have left". Then I saw my whole house like an open doll house, without turning my head! The wallpaper, the borders in the music room, my piano, and all the things I loved.! "And you will be SAFE there" (don't go back to California?). And the time I have left? Then I saw a graphic drawing on the redwood deck something like those hopscotch games we used to draw with chalk on the sidewalk when we were kids. It was there only briefly but it looked like five years with a large year in the middle, two smaller ones, and two pigtails tapering off at the end. Then he said "And I can SEE you whenever I want to!". I screamed out "you can SEE me?" Wow. That's FABULOUS! You're ALIVE! It's a wonder the neighbors didn't hear me, but then, maybe they did. (My neighbor later asked me "if I was alright").

He's alive! He's out there somewhere and ALIVE. In another dimension somewhere. I couldn't see him but he was there. About 3 feet from my lounge and about 3 feet above the deck, sort of under the edge of the roof.

He talked to me. He told me things I needed to know, things that I didn't know. Five years of separation seemed like a long time to endure in my state of misery, but, I thought, "I can't leave now– now that He has blessed me with this information. I wouldn't DARE to leave now. Richard is ALIVE.. I'll stay and be as happy and as useful as I can".

Yes God is good after all, to tell me this, to save my life. I know there is a purpose and a plan for each of us, although we may not know what it is. Three years have gone by and I've done a lot of soul searching, and a lot of growing. I still believe in my epiphany and I know it's true. It helps me to know 'how long' for many reasons. For one thing it helps me with money management. That may sound like a joke but I've heard others say that they don't know how much they can spend because they don't know how long they will live! With Paul unemployed and who knows how long this financial crisis will last?- and with manufacturing jobs having gone overseas, I know he will need money. I was afraid of a prolonged stay in a nursing home which might take all of the family funds and leave Paul out on the sidewalk. Now I know that with my three years of Long Term Insurance it will be enough and there will be something for my heirs. After that I will be gone. I hope Paul manages wisely.

When Jesus arose from the tomb and appeared to Mary on the road, he said, "Do not touch me for I have not yet ascended to my Father".[5] I would supposed this meant that He was in his spiritual body. Richard must've been too. I haven't heard from him since.

* * *

---

[5] John 20:17

"There are more things in heaven and earth than are dreamt of in your philosophy"
Shakespeare

Chapter 34
EPILOGUE

Parapsychology and psychic experience have been studied by scientists and psychologists in well known universities (Duke, Stanford, Univ. of Edinburgh, Scotland) to name a few, beginning with Dr. J. B. Rhine's work at Duke Univ. in 1930. Since that time much responsible lab work has been done producing positive evidence supporting the existence of this unusual phenomena. Scientists are now getting close to explanations, what with Quantum Physics and especially String Theory...the "New Science" which has moved past Einstein's theory of physics and revealed such facts as teleportation and particles which move in and out of existence when given attention! People formerly believed that psychic phenomena were "of the devil",- (you could be burned as a witch)- even though the Bible is full of supernatural events and communications from Angels. Jesus said, in reference to his miracles, "Greater works will you do then I do"[6]. Joan of Arc heard voices from above which directed her to save France. (Hardly the devil). With science studying consciousness, more and more evidence is being found which supports the fact of paranormal occurrences and shows it to be a part of the world which God created, a part that we do not as yet fully understand although scientific research and lab experimentation has caused some scientists to conclude that psychic phenomena is real and that there is a physical reality behind psychic events. The new String theory tells us that all is vibrations,...that all the world is composed of particles, which are also waves, which vibrate. Music is vibrations which some think is the basis of matter, and that the vibrations of two objects, or persons, can remain connected with one another through time and space. This would explain ESP not only here on earth but also communication from 'the other side' when a mind is able to receive due to sensitivity or a former connection,-probably caring.

Nanoparticles existing close to absolute zero move in and out of existence when given attention by scientists who are trying to measure them! Apparently they are on the edge of the universe at the dimension that we can see. Wave frequencies stretch far above and far below our

---

[6] James 14:12

normal sense apprehension; that is, the light spectrum reaches further than what our eyes can see. Consider radio waves, micro-waves, x-rays, infrared, and more. And every person, every brain, vibrates at a unique frequency. Some vibrations attract and some repel. Some make harmony and some make discord.

Dr. Carl Jung, eminent psychiatrist, stated, "In studying the history of the human mind one is impressed that the growth of the mind is a widening of the range of consciousness", meaning growth in awareness, -and thus sensitivity; (the sensitivity needed to receive from the Universal consciousness?)

The cutting edge of science has now become the study of consciousness and what lies beyond it, which may help us to better understand our paranormal experiences. And so I found a psychic dimention hidden within me, activated apparently by love, joy or calamity. I'll bet you have one too.

* * *

Don't stand beside my grave and cry
I am not there; I did not die.

Made in the USA
Charleston, SC
27 November 2009